A LifeBuilder

G000280354

MIRACLES
Signs of God's Glory

12 studies
for individuals or groups

Douglas Connelly

With Notes for Leaders

Scripture Union is an international Christian charity working with churches in more than 130 countries.

Thank you for purchasing this book. Any profits from this book support SU in England and Wales to bring the good news of Jesus Christ to children, young people and families and to enable them to meet God through the Bible and prayer.

Find out more about our work and how you can get involved at:

www.scriptureunion.org.uk (England and Wales)
www.suscotland.org.uk (Scotland)
www.suni.co.uk (Northern Ireland)
www.scriptureunion.org (USA)
www.su.org.au (Australia)

ISBN 978 1 78506 258 2

First published in the United States by InterVarsity Press, 1998.
© Douglas Connelly

Published in the United Kingdom © Scripture Union 1999; this edition 2015, reprinted 2016.

British Library Cataloguing-in-Publication data: a catalogue record for this book is available from the British Library.

Printed in Malta by Gutenberg Press Ltd

Image credit: nicoolay/iStock by Getty Images

Contents

Getting the Most Out of *Miracles*

Most of us could use a miracle. Some physical condition, relational problem or financial crisis in our lives could be solved rather quickly with just one miracle.

When we open the pages of the Bible, our desire for a miracle intensifies as we read astonishing stories of God's power poured out on people just like us. We come away wishing that God would do something supernatural in our lives.

What can we do to experience the power of God unleashed in the struggles and problems we face every day? This study guide will help you discover the answer to that question. Our source of information, however, will not be stories of seemingly miraculous events gleaned from newspapers or inspirational magazines. We will look instead at what God says in his Word about miracles and then try to apply what we learn to the issues we face in our lives today.

I hope you are ready to stand in amazement at God's ability to work in powerful ways. I also hope that you are ready to restructure aspects of your own life. What you learn in these studies will prompt you to pray differently, to face pain and loss differently, and to see God differently than ever before.

Suggestions for Individual Study

1. As you begin each study, pray that God will speak to you through his Word.

2. Read the introduction to the study and respond to the personal reflection question or exercise. This is designed to help you focus on God and on the theme of the study.

3. Each study deals with a particular passage—so that you can delve into the author's meaning in that context. Read and reread the passage to be studied. If you are studying a book, it will be helpful to read through the entire book prior to the first study. The questions are written using the language of the New International Version, so you may wish to use that version of the Bible. The New Revised Standard Version is also recommended.

4. This is an inductive Bible study, designed to help you discover for yourself what Scripture is saying. The study includes three types of questions. *Observation* questions ask about the basic facts: who, what when, where and how. *Interpretation* questions delve into the meaning of the passage. *Application* questions help you discover the implications of the text for growing in Christ. These three keys unlock the treasures of Scripture.

Write your answers to the questions in the spaces provided or in a personal journal. Writing can bring clarity and deeper understanding of yourself and of God's Word.

5. It might be good to have a Bible dictionary handy. Use it to look up any unfamiliar words, names or places.

6. Use the prayer suggestion to guide you in thanking God for what you have learned and to pray about the applications that have come to mind.

7. You may want to go on to the suggestion under "Now or Later," or you may want to use that idea for your next study.

Suggestions for Members of a Group Study

1. Come to the study prepared. Follow the suggestions for individual study mentioned above. You will find that careful preparation will greatly enrich your time spent in group discussion.

2. Be willing to participate in the discussion. The leader of your group will not be lecturing. Instead, he or she will be encouraging the members of the group to discuss what they have learned. The leader will be asking the questions that are found in this guide.

3. Stick to the topic being discussed. Your answers should be based on the verses which are the focus of the discussion and not on outside authorities such as commentaries or speakers. These studies focus on a particular passage of Scripture. Only rarely should you refer to other portions of the Bible. This allows for everyone to participate in in-depth study on equal ground.

4. Be sensitive to the other members of the group. Listen attentively when they describe what they have learned. You may be surprised by their insights! Each question assumes a variety of answers. Many questions do not have "right" answers, particularly questions that aim at meaning or application. Instead the questions push us to explore the passage more thoroughly.

When possible, link what you say to the comments of others. Also, be affirming whenever you can. This will encourage some of the more hesitant members of the group to participate.

5. Be careful not to dominate the discussion. We are sometimes so eager to express our thoughts that we leave too little opportunity for others to respond. By all means participate! But allow others to also.

6. Expect God to teach you through the passage being discussed and through the other members of the group. Pray that you will have an enjoyable and profitable time together, but also that as a result of the study you will find ways that you can take action individually and/or as a group.

7. Remember that anything said in the group is considered confidential and should not be discussed outside the group unless specific permission is given to do so.

8. If you are the group leader, you will find additional suggestions at the back of the guide.

1

Searching for a Sign
Hebrews 2:1-4

We use the word *miracle* in a variety of ways. Every student has uttered those apprehensive words, "If I pass this test, it will be a miracle!" We call it a miracle if we narrowly avoid a car accident or if someone survives a plane crash. Are these really miracles?

GROUP DISCUSSION. What does the word *miracle* mean to you?

Describe a situation from your own experience or from the experience of a friend that you think of as miraculous.

PERSONAL REFLECTION. What miracle in the Bible would you like to have witnessed?

To discover how God has worked in miraculous ways in the past and what our expectations should be about miracles today, we will take a look at how miracles are described in God's Word. We begin with a passage from the book of Hebrews which also gives a glimpse of the purpose of miracles in God's unfolding plan. *Read Hebrews 2:1-4.*

1. The writer of Hebrews is contrasting the commandments of the Old Testament Law given to Moses ("the message spoken by angels") with the message of grace heard now in the gospel. What were the writer's concerns for those who were reading his letter?

2. What was the chain of individuals through which the message of salvation had come from the Lord to the readers of the letter?

3. How was your hearing of the message of salvation in Christ part of that ongoing chain of communication?

4. Those who heard Jesus confirmed the story of Jesus' life, death and resurrection by giving eye-witness accounts of those events (v. 3). Is the message still confirmed to us today? Explain.

5. In what ways did God testify to the truth of the message of salvation (v. 4)?

6. How would you distinguish between *signs, wonders, various miracles* and *gifts of the Holy Spirit*?

7. Do you think the message of the gospel needs to be testified to or authenticated in the same ways today? Explain why or why not.

8. What insight does this passage give you about why Jesus and his early followers performed miracles in the first place?

9. Does this passage lead you to think we should see more miracles today than in Jesus' time or fewer? Explain your answer.

10. Has your confidence in the truthfulness of the gospel message been strengthened by this study? Why or why not?

11. How does the Bible's description of miraculous events compare with how we normally use the word *miracle*?

Ask God to give you a teachable mind and obedient spirit as you explore what the Bible says about miracles.

Now or Later

What are you hoping to receive from these studies on miracles?

What are you willing to invest to get the most from them?

2

Supernatural Wonders in a Scientific Age
Exodus 14:5-31

A few summers ago on a family vacation, we visited one of the beaches along the east coast of the United States. As I stepped into the Atlantic Ocean, the water simply closed in around my feet. The farther I walked from shore, the higher the water rose around me. That is what water normally and predictably does. But at a crucial moment in Israel's history, when it seemed that the entire nation would perish, God powerfully intervened to make a way of escape—through the sea! For hundreds of years after that event, whenever a writer of Scripture wanted to point to the one miracle that demonstrated the awesome ability of God to save his people, he pointed to the deliverance of Israel at the Red Sea.

GROUP DISCUSSION. Describe the most awe-inspiring scene or powerful event in the natural world you have witnessed—a storm, an earthquake, the power of the ocean. How did you feel as you watched or experienced that event?

PERSONAL REFLECTION. Think of a powerful work of God that you have experienced. Respond with genuine adoration and awe to the God who loves to surprise you with his creative power.

---

1. *Read Exodus 14:5-31.* Imagine yourself as part of this scene. What different emotions would have gripped your heart as you saw these events unfold?

---

2. What resources did the Egyptians have for their pursuit of the Israelites?

What resources did the Israelites have to defend themselves?

---

3. What did God want the people of Israel to learn through this experience (vv. 10-14)?

---

4. What insights can you glean from Moses' words in verses 13 and 14 that will help you face difficult times in your own life?

---

5. Do the complaints of the people of Israel (vv. 11-12) sound like complaints we raise to God in times of panic or difficulty? Give an example from personal experience.

6. How did God "gain glory" through the destruction of Pharaoh and his army (vv. 17-18)?

---

7. Attempts have been made to find a "natural" explanation for what happened at the Red Sea. What elements in the story might suggest natural explanations for Israel's escape?

What aspects of the story clearly point to a supernatural explanation?

What is your conclusion about this account? Explain. (Was this the intervention of God or just fortunate circumstances?)

---

8. God uses Moses prominently in the performance of this miracle (vv. 21, 26, 31). What light might Moses' role shed on the purpose for God's miracles in general?

---

9. In what ways has God rescued you?

How does that compare with the power God displays in this passage?

Praise God for delivering you from the bondage of the old life and giving you new life in Christ.

Now or Later

The people of Israel celebrated God's victory over his enemies with a song of praise (Exodus 15:1-21). Use your own creativity to praise God for his deliverance and power in your life. Compose a song, write a prayer, express your worship in dance (Exodus 15:20), use photography or painting to display the awesome power of God. God has given us countless avenues for expressing our adoration to him.

3

Jesus the Miracle Worker

Luke 7:11-23

I grew up in a Christian family. I heard about Jesus from my earliest days and believed in him when I was a young boy. In my first years of college, however, I began to have some doubts about Jesus and the Bible. Was Jesus really who I thought he was? Was he the Lord of glory or just a good man?

My own doubts forced me to dig for answers. I didn't want the pat answers I had accepted up until then. I wanted tough answers that could stand up to the relentless questioning of a university professor or a secular culture. I emerged from my doubts with a stronger commitment than ever to Christ. God gave me room to doubt and then demonstrated himself stronger than any critic's attack.

GROUP DISCUSSION. What political leader, religious figure or family member have you lost faith in? What would it take to restore your confidence in that person?

PERSONAL REFLECTION. What evidence persuaded you to believe in Jesus as Savior and Lord?

In the middle of Jesus' ministry one of Jesus' strongest supporters found himself struggling with doubt. John the Baptizer had announced the soon arrival of Israel's Deliverer and had pointed to Jesus as the one they were waiting for. But now John sat in prison (Luke 3:20). *Read Luke 7:11-23.*

1. What reports would John have heard about Jesus (vv. 11-17)?

2. Why would John's circumstances prompt him to ask Jesus the question in verse 19?

3. Do you think it would have been more effective if Jesus had just answered John's question with words of explanation? Why or why not?

4. Jesus didn't seem frustrated by John's question—or disappointed in him. What insight does that give you about how Jesus responds to you when you have doubts?

5. Do you think Jesus' reply (vv. 22-23) resolved John's doubts? Explain your answer.

6. Why didn't Jesus perform a miracle to set John free from his prison or to strike down John's oppressors?

7. According to this passage why did Jesus perform miracles during his ministry?

8. What effect (if any) would an outpouring of spectacular miracles have on our society today?

9. How would you respond to Christians who say we should see the same intensity of miraculous activity today that we read about in this passage?

How would you respond to Christians who say that all miraculous activity has ceased?

10. When you read about Jesus' miracles, how does that affect your view of him and his power in your life?

Thank God that even when we doubt him he continues to love us and demonstrate his power in our lives.

Now or Later

Think of one person you want to tell that you are a follower of Jesus Christ. Plan what you will say and then look for the right opportunity to express your beliefs. Make yourself accountable to your study group or to a Christian friend to do it.

4

Power in the Presence of Death

Luke 8:40-42, 49-56

+ Mark 5:21 - 43

After a tour in the military my older brother worked for a while as an orderly in a hospital emergency room. He was told one day to take a man's body down to the morgue. My brother finished what he was doing and then went to move the man's transport bed. Without thinking about it my brother took the man's wrist to check his pulse. It only took a few seconds for him to realize what he was doing, and he put the man's arm back on the bed—but not before his fingers felt a slight pulse! The doctors were called, and the man on his way to the morgue lived on.

Eight people in the Bible were miraculously raised back to life after death. In contrast to the man in the hospital, these eight really died first and then were raised to life by God's power.

GROUP DISCUSSION. What do you think about people who claim to have died and come back to life?

PERSONAL REFLECTION. How do you respond to a desperate situation?

1. *Read Luke 8:40-42, 49-56. Picture yourself as Jairus, the girl's father.* What emotions would you have experienced over the course of this encounter with Jesus?

2. Do you think the girl really died or not? What evidence from the passage supports your conclusion?

3. When Jairus was told that his daughter had already died, Jesus told him not to be afraid (v. 50). Describe a time you have been too fearful to bring a problem to God.

" Faide is being curtin of what you hope for, sure of what you cannot see -

4. Jesus also told Jairus, "Just believe" (v. 50). What place does faith have in this miracle?

5. Contrast Jairus' response to Jesus with the response of the "mourners" in the house.

6. How would you answer the skeptics who laugh at the suggestion of

God's miraculous power today?

—————————————————————

✗ 7. Why did Jesus tell the girl's parents not to tell anyone what had happened? (Wouldn't the fact that the girl was alive make it obvious that Jesus had raised her?)

—————————————————————

✗ 8. Do you think we should ask God to bring back to life a Christian who has died? Why or why not?

—————————————————————

✗ 9. When have you been as desperate or fearful as Jairus was?

How did Jesus touch your life in that situation?

—————————————————————

✗ 10. How will this study help you to begin to pray differently about difficult problems that arise in your life?

Ask God to remind you in desperate situations that he is the source of peace and power.

Now or Later

✗⇏ What act of compassion and kindness can you show this week to someone who is ill or grieving?

❉❉Will you be disappointed if the person doesn't tell other people about
your kindness?

5

Rebuking
Satan's Power

Luke 8:26-39

A very unusual visitor came into our church one Sunday morning. As I walked across the foyer to greet the man, a chill ran down my back. I introduced myself and tried to carry on a conversation with him but my mind and my spirit were repelled by his very presence. Evil seemed to radiate from him.

As I walked into the auditorium to begin the worship service, I found myself deeply disturbed by this man's presence in our church. I had never experienced anything like it. I had welcomed skeptics, atheists, Muslims, Buddhists and plenty of plain old pagans into our services, and I had rejoiced to see them come. But this man was different.

I sat down on a front pew and simply asked God to hinder any evil presence from disrupting our worship. I also prayed that the presentation of the gospel would penetrate this man's heart. The oppression I felt was lifted, and we worshiped the Lord without interruption.

I watched the man as I preached, not out of fear but to see his response to God's truth. He looked with disdain at all that went on around him and walked out as the final prayer was spoken. I am convinced that he was under the control of a powerful demon.

GROUP DISCUSSION. Have you ever been in a situation in which you sensed an evil presence or power? If so, what were the circumstances and how did you respond?

PERSONAL REFLECTION. If you could be free of just one thing, what would it be?

Jesus was confronted one day by a man screaming in agony. Behind his screams, however, Jesus sensed another presence—the presence of an evil spirit. *Read Luke 8:26-39.*

1. As you look through the passage again, describe how you would have felt standing at Jesus' side during this encounter.

2. What had this man's life been like before he met Jesus (vv. 27-29)?

3. How did Jesus treat the man differently from the way the people of the area had treated him?

4. How do you think most people today would diagnose this man's problem?

5. Was Jesus' reference to an "evil spirit" in the man (v. 29) simply an accommodation to popular belief or was there really an evil power controlling the man? What evidence in the passage itself supports your position?

6. Do you think evil spirits or demons are active in our world today? Why or why not?

7. What were the people of the region afraid of when they asked Jesus to leave (v. 37)?

8. Jesus responded positively to every request—to the demons' plea, to the people's request for him to leave. The only person Jesus turned down was the liberated man who wanted to come with him. Why did Jesus say no to him and what resulted instead?

9. Do you think Christians today have the same authority over demons that Jesus exercised in Luke 8? Explain your answer.

10. What principles should guide us as we identify and confront demonic power?

11. Do you feel more secure or more threatened in your spiritual life as you come to the end of this study? Why?

Thank God for his protection from evil powers. Ask him to help you grow stronger in your faith in him as a shield against Satan's attacks.

Now or Later

Read Ephesians 6:10-18. What spiritual resources are available to us in our struggle against Satan's evil power?

Which of these resources need to be strengthened in your own life?

6

When Our
Efforts Fail

Mark 9:14-29

Soon after construction began on an addition to our church building, a man stopped by to ask me why we were enlarging our facility. I told him that our congregation had grown and we needed classrooms for our children's ministries.

"What's your secret?" was the next question. "Our church is shrinking. How can we get it to grow?" I sensed that behind his question was a deeper problem than a declining congregation. He was asking if there wasn't some trick, some program, some slick technique to bring people in. He had bought into the delusion that if we would just put our minds to it, we could build Christ's kingdom on our own.

GROUP DISCUSSION. Divide the group into smaller groups of three or more. Give each group one magazine, one newspaper section, one pencil, one ten-inch piece of string and five paper clips, giving at least one item to each person. The groups are to create towers from their material—the group with the highest tower wins. Each person has the power to decide how to use their item. Allow six minutes for construction. Measure the towers and declare the winner. Then talk about your experience in working together. (Did all contribute? Did one person dominate? How did it feel to win or lose?)

PERSONAL REFLECTION. How do you respond to failure in your life?

How do you respond to failure in others?

Some of Jesus' disciples tried one day to accomplish in their own strength what only God could do—and they failed miserably. *Read Mark 9:14-29.*

---

1. Jesus speaks five times in the sound track of this passage—to the crowd (v. 19), to the disciples and scribes (v. 16), to the boy's father (vv. 21, 23), to the evil spirit (v. 25) and to the disciples alone (v. 29). What tone of voice can you imagine Jesus using in each case?

---

2. What do you think the disciples had already done in their attempts to deal with the demon-possessed boy?

---

3. Describe what the evil spirit had done to the boy.

---

4. Jesus responded to the disciples' inability to cast out the demon by including them in the "*unbelieving* generation" (v. 19). When the father wondered about Jesus' ability to remove the demon, Jesus encouraged him to "believe" (v. 23). Why was faith so important in this situation?

5. Think of a situation in your life that seems impossible to resolve or change. What attempts have you made to alter the situation and what have been the results?

6. What possibilities about your situation come to mind when you read Jesus' statement that "everything is possible to him who believes" (v. 23)?

7. How might it be possible to misuse Jesus' statement in verse 23 in your own life or in the life of another person?

8. Many present-day miracle workers would condemn the boy's father for his weak response (v. 24) to Jesus' encouragement to believe. Why doesn't Jesus rebuke him?

9. What doubts and fears come to your mind when you think about turning problem situations over to the Lord?

10. When the disciples asked Jesus why they had failed to drive the demon out, Jesus said, "This kind can come out only by prayer" (v. 29). But there is no record that Jesus prayed as he rebuked the demon. Had the disciples simply failed to pray or was there more to Jesus' statement? Explain your answer.

11. Based on your study of this passage what spiritual disciplines can you cultivate that will prompt you to rely more readily on God's wisdom and power?

12. What direction can you give a friend, a group of friends or church leaders who feel powerless?

Ask God for his wisdom and intervention in the areas of temptation you face.

Now or Later

Read the accounts of this same miracle in Matthew 17:14-20 and Luke 9:37-43. What additional insights do these parallel passages provide into Jesus' rebuke of his disciples? the response of the crowd to Jesus' miracle?

7

Facing an Impossible Situation

John 6:1-15

The man in my office sat with his head in his hands. His voice was choked with emotion. His daughter was an addict. He and his wife had tried for years to rescue her. They had paid for counseling and months in a rehab center. They had taken her back into their home only to have money stolen and to find her later at their front door stoned. The man's wife had come to the end of her tolerance. She had also given him an ultimatum—cut ties with the daughter or face a divorce. His heart was being torn in two. His situation seemed impossible. Before he left, we prayed that God would do a miracle.

GROUP DISCUSSION. Bring several small "impossible" puzzles (Rubic's cube, twisted steel rings) and take turns trying to solve them. Discuss how you respond to impossible tasks and situations.

PERSONAL REFLECTION. Think about the situations or circumstances in which you have a difficult time trusting in God and his love for you.

How do you respond in those situations?

Jesus faced many difficult and challenging situations during his earthly ministry, but one of his greatest challenges must have been the day when he looked up to see a huge crowd of hungry people coming toward him. *Read John 6:1-15.*

1. How did the crowd's attitude toward Jesus change over the course of this event?

2. How would you characterize Philip's and Andrew's response to the problem of feeding this enormous crowd?

3. Is your personal response to a difficult situation more like Philip's or more like Andrew's? Explain and give an example.

4. If Jesus knew what he was going to do (v. 6), why did he ask these two disciples for advice?

5. Imagine yourself as one of Jesus' disciples. What would be going through your mind as you passed out the food and then gathered up the pieces that were left?

6. Why did Jesus respond to the crowd's intention by withdrawing (v. 15)?

What does Jesus' response tell you about his idea of what his kingship in a person's life should be like?

_____

7. What insight does this account give you into how the Lord may be at work in the difficult situations in your life?

_____

8. What counsel from this passage can you give to a friend who is facing a seemingly impossible situation?

_____

9. If we give a problem situation over to the Lord, will he always solve it miraculously? Explain.

What other options might God use to come to our aid?

Thank God for his care and provision for you. Ask him to remind you of his presence and power when you are in difficult situations.

Now or Later

Write out some of the promises of God that assure you of his love and care. Put those promises in places where you tend to do your worrying—on the dashboard of your car, inside your checkbook, next to your bed. Some verses you might consider are: Isaiah 41:10; 24:3-4; Psalm 4:8; Philippians 4:6-7; Hebrews 13:5. The next time you find yourself in a difficult situation, focus on God's promises. The problem will look a lot different from a new perspective.

8

"Do You Want to Get Well?"

If I could have one ability that Jesus had during his earthly ministry, I would choose the ability to heal the sick. I can think of very few things in the human realm more rewarding than restoring the health of a cancer victim or making a child who is stricken with cystic fibrosis whole again. I often find myself visiting a hospital room or sitting in the home of a dying friend wishing I had the capacity to bring instant healing to that person's weak and ravaged body.

GROUP DISCUSSION. What are you like when you get sick?
☐ a whimpering puppy
☐ a roaring lion
☐ a hibernating bear
How do people around you usually respond when you are sick?

PERSONAL REFLECTION. When have you experienced physical pain that you longed for Jesus to heal?

Twenty specific miracles of healing are recorded in the Gospels. Each one reveals Jesus' power and compassion. Jesus changed many lives but few were changed as dramatically as the life of a man who had waited thirty-eight years for a miracle. *Read John 5:1-15.*

1. If you were a CNN reporter covering this story, what scenes would you include in your video report?

What people would you interview? Why?

2. What was Jesus trying to discover about the man at the pool when he asked him, "Do you want to get well?" (v. 6)?

3. Was the man's response to Jesus (v. 7) an explanation or an excuse? Why did you come to that conclusion?

4. When have you felt that God was waiting too long to do what you had asked him to do?

5. The man was cured instantly. How did the people around him respond (vv. 9-10)?

6. The healed man did not even know who Jesus was (v. 13). What insight does that give you on the relationship between a person's faith and miraculous healing?

_____

7. When Jesus talked to the man later (v. 14), he told him to "stop sinning or something worse may happen to you." Do you think the man was physically sick because of sin in his life? Explain.

_____

8. If Jesus is the same today as he was when he was on earth, should we expect the same dramatic healings today? Why or why not?

_____

9. Based on the principles gleaned from this incident, what will you do the next time you are sick?

_____

10. What advice and direction will you give to a Christian friend who becomes sick or disabled?

What are some things you will _not_ say?

Acknowledge to God that he alone is the one who heals (Exodus 15:26).

Now or Later

Talk to a Christian friend who has experienced serious sickness. Ask the friend what promises from Scripture he or she found most sustaining during the rough times. What spiritual disciplines (prayer, meditation, worship) brought comfort? Remember that you are not talking with the person to sit in judgment but to learn from someone who has walked the path of suffering.

9

When the Wrong Seems Strong

John and Betty Stam had been married only fourteen months when Communist insurgents forced their way into their mission home in the Chinese province of Anhwei. On December 8, 1934, two days after their capture, the young couple was bound with ropes and led down the street where they had witnessed about Jesus Christ and his saving grace. On a hill outside the town John began to speak again of his love for Christ when the executioner ended his testimony by cutting his throat. His wife Betty fell to her knees beside him. A flash of the sword reunited the couple in heaven's glory.

It might surprise you to know that the century in which most Christians have died for their faith is not the first or second century, when Christians were slaughtered in Roman amphitheaters. The century most stained by the blood of Christians is the twentieth century—and the twenty-first doesn't show many signs of improvement. Where is God when evil seems victorious?

GROUP DISCUSSION. If the government told you that you could not pray, carry a Bible or meet for worship with other Christians, what would you do?

PERSONAL REFLECTION. Think of a time when you have been ridiculed or mocked because of your commitment to Jesus Christ or your belief in biblical values. How did you respond?

The early Christian community faced an incredible challenge when their leaders were rounded up and put in jail. *Read Acts 5:17-32.*

1. What thoughts filled the minds of the apostles when they were first arrested?

when the angel set them free?

when they were arrested again (v. 26)?

2. The angel told them to continue witnessing in public (v. 20). What would your response have been to the angel's command under the same circumstances?

3. What do you learn about how the apostles view the authorities from verses 28-32?

4. Who or what is the ultimate authority in your life?

In what specific, observable ways do you demonstrate your allegiance to that authority?

---

5. What do we learn about God's work in Jesus that can bring us comfort in the face of persecution (vv. 29-32)?

---

6. Why does God sometimes deliver us out of difficult situations but at other times allow us to go through them?

---

7. When you hear of Christians being persecuted or killed for their faith, does it make you question God's love or God's power? Explain.

---

8. Based on your study of this passage, how would you comfort or strengthen a Christian sister or brother under persecution or arrest?

---

9. What steps can you take to be more courageous in demonstrating your allegiance to Christ?

What other Christian can you ask to hold you accountable for implementing these steps in your life?

Pray for Christians who are suffering persecution for their faith.

Now or Later

Check out some of the organizations that monitor and provide information on the persecution of Christians around the world. You can find them easily on the Internet. Periodicals like *Christianity Today* regularly feature articles about the oppressed church. Your pastor may also be able to direct you to some persecution-monitoring organizations. Become more informed about persecuted Christians, and commit yourself to some level of personal involvement on their behalf.

10

Deceptive Miracles & Miracle Workers

Matthew 7:15-27

Several years ago a man in my congregation told me that he was planning to attend a healing service in a city a few miles away. A local pastor had gained quite a reputation in our area with his claims that Christians didn't need doctors or medicine or even eyeglasses! All we needed was faith—and the touch of his miracle-working hands. I counseled my friend not to go, but he was dying of cancer and was desperate for a cure.

The cancer took my friend's life a few months later. It took another year for the miracle-worker's ministry to collapse. He became more and more cultic in his proclamations and (as it turned out) more and more corrupt in his personal life. In time the huge auditorium his followers had built for him was boarded up.

GROUP DISCUSSION. Are you more likely to trust or distrust people you have just met? Are you more often right or wrong in your initial evaluation?

PERSONAL REFLECTION. What inner alarm alerts you when a person is a phony? How do you respond when you have been deceived by an advertisement or by another person?

How do we know if someone who claims miraculous power is really from God? Is a person's use of the name of Jesus enough? Jesus addresses the issue of those who claim to work miracles in his name and what he says may surprise you. *Read Matthew 7:15-27.*

1. Jesus draws several sets of contrasts in this passage. What are they and which one speaks most powerfully to you?

2. In verse 1 of Matthew 7 Jesus tells us not to judge each other, but in verse 15 he says to watch out for false prophets. Does the command to evaluate the fruit of someone's ministry contradict the command not to judge? Explain your answer.

3. What is the "fruit" that we are to use in evaluating a person's ministry (vv. 16-20)?

4. What would lead you to believe that the people in verses 21-22 are genuine servants of God?

5. Why does Jesus banish these same people from his kingdom and call them evildoers (v. 23)?

---

6. If miracles performed in Jesus' name are not considered enough to verify a person's ministry, what else should we look for?

---

7. Do you think the average Christian is too gullible or too critical of the leadership in his or her local church?

What about toward the claims of a celebrity television preacher?

---

8. What hints can you find in Jesus' commendation of the wise man (vv. 24-25) that will help you evaluate a person's ministry properly?

---

9. What principles can you glean from this passage that will help you become more biblically discerning toward ministries that claim to be done in the name of Christ?

---

10. If other believers would honestly evaluate your Christian character and ministry, what would they conclude about you?

What specific steps can you take this week to strengthen your own testimony and ministry to others?

Ask God to help you find the balance between a healthy sense of discernment and a joyful, receptive attitude toward other Christians.

Now or Later

Is your need at this point to learn more about what Jesus and the Bible teach or to put into practice what you already know?

How can the members of your study group or church help you pursue that goal?

11

Convincing the Skeptic

Matthew 12:22-37

I can't read the Gospels without wishing I had been alive when Jesus was on earth. I've wondered what it would have been like to spend time in Jesus' company, to hear him teach, to watch his miracles of power. From what the Gospel writers tell us, most of the people who saw Jesus at work were astonished by his miracles. A few, however, had a very different reaction.

It might surprise you to know that none of Jesus' enemies ever denied the *reality* of his miracles. Instead they debated the *source* of Jesus' power. His miraculous works (they said) came not from God but from Satan. That accusation moved them onto dangerous spiritual ground.

GROUP DISCUSSION. Ask someone in the group to play the role of the skeptic. The other members of the group have the responsibility of persuading the "skeptic" that the miracles credited to Jesus in the Gospels really happened. After five or six minutes of debate, evaluate the process. Which arguments seemed most persuasive? Was the "skeptic" swayed by the arguments or not?

PERSONAL REFLECTION. What questions do you have about Jesus and his miracles?

---

1. *Read Matthew 12:22-37.* If the events in these verses were videotaped by a news crew, which clips would make the evening broadcast?

Which parts would probably be eliminated?

---

2. The people who witnessed this miracle began to wonder if Jesus was, in fact, the Messiah. "Could this be the Son of David?" (v. 23). Why did that arouse suspicion in the religious leaders?

---

3. What would have been required of the Pharisees if they had acknowledged that Jesus performed his miracles by God's power instead of Beelzebub's (a vulgar name for Satan)?

---

4. What are some of the ways modern skeptics explain (or explain away) Jesus' miracles?

5. Jesus used three lines of defense to answer their accusation (vv. 26, 27, 29). Write out his arguments in your own words.

_____

6. What alternative explanation of his miracles does Jesus give to the Pharisees' accusation (v. 28)?

_____

7. How would the fact that "the kingdom of God has come upon you" affect the power and influence of the Pharisees?

_____

8. The accusation these people raised against Jesus was unique in history. Never before had God the Son, now fully human, by the power of God's Spirit performed such undeniable authenticating signs. Why does Jesus say their sin will not be forgiven (vv. 31-32)?

_____

9. According to verses 33-35, what did the evil words spoken by the Pharisees reveal about them?

_____

10. What insight does the unwillingness of these Pharisees to believe in Jesus give you as you talk to people who deny or attack what the Bible says about Jesus?

11. What specific changes can you make in your life that will show that you take Jesus' warning in verses 36 and 37 seriously?

Ask God to help you to be wise and courageous when you are challenged by those who do not believe in Christ.

Now or Later

List the questions that skeptics usually raise about Jesus or the Bible—was Jesus really God? Is the Bible trustworthy? Don't all religions lead to heaven? Choose one question and formulate a biblical response.

If you want to follow Jesus' pattern from the passage in this study, he (1) addressed the faulty logic behind their accusation, (2) pointed out that their real problem was unbelief, and (3) called them to put their trust in him for forgiveness and eternal life.

Once you have developed a response, be prepared to use it!

12

When God
Says No

"Our God is a God of miracles!" We say those words to other people who are in crisis. We certainly believe the words. But when the trial comes in its fury into our lives, and especially when the suffering seems to have no end, we are tempted to wonder if God is really as powerful as we thought he was. "If God really loves me," we ask, "why doesn't he do something?"

What can we do until the miracle comes? And what if it *never* comes? Maybe you have prayed for healing and trusted God but the cancer keeps spreading. You have committed your son to the Lord and passionately prayed for God's intervention, but he continues to pursue a lifestyle that cannot please God. The business debt continues to grow and your best efforts have not turned it around. Christian counselors and a shelf full of books have not stopped your marriage or your parents' marriage from crumbling. What now?

GROUP DISCUSSION. What "miracle" could you use in your life right now?

PERSONAL REFLECTION. Take a few minutes to present your need before God in prayer. Tell God about any pain you feel. Be assured that God is listening.

We can gain some profound insight for our own lives as we read the apostle Paul's prayer for a miracle that doesn't come. *Read 2 Corinthians 12:1-10.*

---

1. If you drew an emotional chart of this passage, where would you locate the high points? What are the low points?

---

2. Was Paul writing about himself in verses 2-5 or about someone else? How did you come to your conclusion?

---

3. What do you think Paul means when he describes a "thorn" in his flesh (v. 7)?

---

4. How would that thorn keep Paul from becoming conceited?

---

5. How do you think Paul felt when on each of the three separate occasions in which he pleaded with God to remove the thorn, God said "No"?

---

6. How do you react when God says no to your urgent requests?

How would you respond if God gave you the answer he gave Paul in verse 9?

_____

7. What help does this incident give you in understanding why God may *not* bring healing or a miracle into your situation?

_____

8. Describe a time of weakness in your life when God has shown himself to be strong.

_____

9. Is it easier for you to trust a God who will always miraculously deliver you from sickness and suffering, or a God who stays with you through the difficulty? Why?

_____

10. What counsel can you give to a Christian friend who is struggling with a physical or emotional crisis?

What can you say to a Christian who says that he or she has prayed fervently but God didn't (or won't) answer?

Ask God to remind you of his promises and his abundant supply of grace when you are going through a difficult time.

Now or Later

As you reflect back over these studies, what principles from Scripture have made the deepest impressions on your mind and heart? Write the principles and appropriate passages of Scripture in your journal or on one of the blank pages at the front or back of your Bible. When you are suffering, read through the principles and promises of God. Rest in his grace. And when God delivers you, stand in wonder at his great power.

Leader's Notes

Leading a Bible discussion can be an enjoyable and rewarding experience. But it can also be *scary*—especially if you've never done it before. If this is your feeling, you're in good company. When God asked Moses to lead the Israelites out of Egypt, he replied, "O Lord, please send someone else to do it!" (Ex 4:13). It was the same with Solomon, Jeremiah and Timothy, but God helped these people in spite of their weaknesses, and he will help you as well.

You don't need to be an expert on the Bible or a trained teacher to lead a Bible discussion. The idea behind these inductive studies is that the leader guides group members to discover for themselves what the Bible has to say. This method of learning will allow group members to remember much more of what is said than a lecture would.

These studies are designed to be led easily. As a matter of fact, the flow of questions through the passage from observation to interpretation to application is so natural that you may feel that the studies lead themselves. This study guide is also flexible. You can use it with a variety of groups—student, professional, neighborhood or church groups. Each study takes forty-five to sixty minutes in a group setting.

There are some important facts to know about group dynamics and encouraging discussion. The suggestions listed below should enable you to effectively and enjoyably fulfill your role as leader.

Preparing for the Study

1. Ask God to help you understand and apply the passage in your own life. Unless this happens, you will not be prepared to lead others. Pray too for the various members of the group. Ask God to open your hearts to the

message of his Word and motivate you to action.

2. Read the introduction to the entire guide to get an overview of the entire book and the issues which will be explored.

3. As you begin each study, read and reread the assigned Bible passage to familiarize yourself with it.

4. This study guide is based on the New International Version of the Bible. It will help you and the group if you use this translation as the basis for your study and discussion.

5. Carefully work through each question in the study. Spend time in meditation and reflection as you consider how to respond.

6. Write your thoughts and responses in the space provided in the study guide. This will help you to express your understanding of the passage clearly.

7. It might help to have a Bible dictionary handy. Use it to look up any unfamiliar words, names or places. (For additional help on how to study a passage, see chapter five of *Leading Bible Discussions*, InterVarsity Press.)

8. Consider how you can apply the Scripture to your life. Remember that the group will follow your lead in responding to the studies. They will not go any deeper than you do.

9. Once you have finished your own study of the passage, familiarize yourself with the leader's notes for the study you are leading. These are designed to help you in several ways. First, they tell you the purpose the study guide author had in mind when writing the study. Take time to think through how the study questions work together to accomplish that purpose. Second, the notes provide you with additional background information or suggestions on group dynamics for various questions. This information can be useful when people have difficulty understanding or answering a question. Third, the leader's notes can alert you to potential problems you may encounter during the study.

10. If you wish to remind yourself of anything mentioned in the leader's notes, make a note to yourself below that question in the study.

Leading the Study

1. Begin the study on time. Open with prayer, asking God to help the group to understand and apply the passage.

2. Be sure that everyone in your group has a study guide. Encourage the

group to prepare beforehand for each discussion by reading the introduction to the guide and by working through the questions in the study.

3. At the beginning of your first time together, explain that these studies are meant to be discussions, not lectures. Encourage the members of the group to participate. However, do not put pressure on those who may be hesitant to speak during the first few sessions. You may want to suggest the following guidelines to your group.

☐ Stick to the topic being discussed.

☐ Your responses should be based on the verses which are the focus of the discussion and not on outside authorities such as commentaries or speakers.

☐ These studies focus on a particular passage of Scripture. Only rarely should you refer to other portions of the Bible. This allows for everyone to participate in in-depth study on equal ground.

☐ Anything said in the group is considered confidential and will not be discussed outside the group unless specific permission is given to do so.

☐ We will listen attentively to each other and provide time for each person present to talk.

☐ We will pray for each other.

4. Have a group member read the introduction at the beginning of the discussion.

5. Every session begins with a group discussion question. The question or activity is meant to be used before the passage is read. The question introduces the theme of the study and encourages group members to begin to open up. Encourage as many members as possible to participate and be ready to get the discussion going with your own response.

This section is designed to reveal where our thoughts or feelings need to be transformed by Scripture. That is why it is especially important not to read the passage before the discussion question is asked. The passage will tend to color the honest reactions people would otherwise give because they are, of course, supposed to think the way the Bible does.

You may want to supplement the group discussion question with an icebreaker to help people to get comfortable. See the community section of *Small Group Idea Book* for more ideas.

You also might want to use the personal reflection question with your group. Either allow a time of silence for people to respond individually or discuss it together.

6. Have a group member (or members if the passage is long) read aloud the passage to be studied. Then give people several minutes to read the passage again silently so that they can take it all in.

7. Question 1 will generally be an overview question designed to briefly survey the passage. Encourage the group to briefly survey the passage, but try to avoid getting sidetracked by questions or issues that will be addressed later in the study.

8. As you ask the questions, keep in mind that they are designed to be used just as they are written. You may simply read them aloud. Or you may prefer to express them in your own words.

There may be times when it is appropriate to deviate from the study guide. For example, a question may have already been answered. If so, move on to the next question. Or someone may raise an important question not covered in the guide. Take time to discuss it, but try to keep the group from going off on tangents.

9. Avoid answering your own questions. If necessary, repeat or rephrase them until they are clearly understood. Or point out something you read in the leader's notes to clarify the context or meaning. An eager group quickly becomes passive and silent if they think the leader will do most of the talking.

10. Don't be afraid of silence. People may need time to think about the question before formulating their answers.

11. Don't be content with just one answer. Ask, "What do the rest of you think?" or "Anything else?" until several people have given answers to the question.

12. Acknowledge all contributions. Try to be affirming whenever possible. Never reject an answer. If it is clearly off-base, ask, "Which verse led you to that conclusion?" or again, "What do the rest of you think?"

13. Don't expect every answer to be addressed to you, even though this will probably happen at first. As group members become more at ease, they will begin to truly interact with each other. This is one sign of healthy discussion.

14. Don't be afraid of controversy. It can be very stimulating. If you don't resolve an issue completely, don't be frustrated. Move on and keep it in mind for later. A subsequent study may solve the problem.

15. Periodically summarize what the group has said about the passage This helps to draw together the various ideas mentioned and gives continuity to the study. But don't preach.

16. At the end of the Bible discussion you may want to allow group members a time of quiet to work on an idea under "Now or Later." Then discuss what you experienced. Or you may want to encourage group members to work on these ideas between meetings. Give an opportunity during the session to allow people to talk about what they are learning.

17. Conclude your time together with conversational prayer, adapting the prayer suggestion at the end of the study to your group. Ask for God's help in following through on the commitments you've made.

18. End on time.

Many more suggestions and helps are found in *Leading Bible Discussions*, which is part of the LifeGuide Bible Study series.

Components of Small Groups

A healthy small group should do more than study the Bible. There are four components to consider as you structure your time together.

Nurture. Small groups help us to grow in our knowledge and love of God. Bible study is the key to making this happen and is the foundation of your small group.

Community. Small groups are a great place to develop deep friendships with other Christians. Allow time for informal interaction before and after each study. Plan activities and games that will help you to get to know each other. Spend time having fun together—going on a picnic or cooking dinner together.

Worship and prayer. Your study will be enhanced by spending time praising God together in prayer or song. Pray for each other's needs—and keep track of how God is answering prayer in your group. Ask God to help you to apply what you are learning in your study.

Outreach. Reaching out to others can be a practical way of applying what you are learning, and it will keep your group from becoming self-focused. Host a series of evangelistic discussions for your friends or neighbors. Clean up the yard of an elderly friend. Serve at a soup kitchen together, or spend a day working on a Habitat house.

Many more suggestions and helps in each of these areas are found in

Small Group Idea Book. Information on building a small group can be found in *Small Group Leaders' Handbook* and *The Big Book on Small Groups* (both from InterVarsity Press). Reading through one of these books would be worth your time.

Study 1. Searching for a Sign. Hebrews 2:1-4.

Purpose: To discover the purpose of miracles in God's redemptive plan.

General note. A study on miracles can be a source of great encouragement—and great controversy. Ask the members of your group to come to these studies with teachable minds and humble spirits. Some of their most cherished beliefs and opinions may be challenged!

As a group leader it will be helpful for you to have some broader insight into the biblical teaching on miracles. My book *Miracles: What the Bible Says* (InterVarsity Press, 1997) will introduce the various kinds of miracles and will give you one perspective on the purpose of miracles in the plan of God. If you want a good defense of the reality of biblical miracles, read Norman Geisler, *Miracles and the Modern Mind: A Defense of Biblical Miracles* (Baker, 1992) or R. Douglas Geivett and Gary R. Habermas, eds., *In Defense of Miracles,* (InterVarsity Press, 1997).

Group discussion. The aim of this question is not to pass judgment on whether a person's experience was miraculous or not. The goal is to explore what events the people in your group consider to be miraculous.

Question 1. See Deuteronomy 33:2 for the role of the angels in giving the law.

The writer of Hebrews argues that if violation of the law brought certain punishment, then disregard for the message of the gospel would bring even more severe consequences. The writer of this letter assumes that the gospel is greater than the law. He is concerned that some in his "congregation" were drifting away from Christ as the only source of salvation.

Question 2. Three key links in the chain of transmission are (1) "the Lord" (referring to Jesus), (2) "those who heard him" (the apostles, the twelve closest disciples who were specifically chosen to be leaders of the early church) and (3) "us" (those who had believed on Christ through the testimony of the apostles). The writer of Hebrews can be viewed as the fourth link in the chain, since the writer brought the message to the people who first read his letter.

Question 4. We have the same reliable eyewitness accounts available in the Gospels. The message is confirmed today by the Holy Spirit who convinces those who hear the gospel of its truthfulness. We believe the message by faith as we are convinced in our hearts of its reality.

Question 6. The words used in verse 4 all point to miraculous works but each word has a slightly different emphasis. If the group has trouble answering the question, you might point them to some of the passages referenced below.

A *sign* is a miraculous work of God that has special meaning. Jesus' miracles, for example, were designed by God to point to Jesus as the Messiah, Israel's promised Redeemer (Jn 20:30-31). Moses was given three signs, three miracles, designed to point to Moses as God's true representative to his people (Ex 4:1-9).

God's miracles are also designed to produce astonishment or *wonder* in those who experience them or hear about them. The appropriate response to God's miraculous work is to marvel at what he has done.

The phrase *various miracles* is literally "various works of power." Miracles demonstrate God's power. No human being is ever given credit for a genuine miracle.

Gifts of the Holy Spirit is most likely a reference to the more spectacular gifts given in Acts as authentication of the gospel message and the coming of the Holy Spirit in a new way upon believers. In Acts 2 the followers of Jesus spoke "in other tongues as the Spirit enabled them" (Acts 2:4). Cornelius and his household believed the gospel and received the same baptism of the Spirit (Acts 10:44-45; 11:15-17). The proof that the Spirit had come upon them was that they were "speaking in tongues and praising God" (Acts 10:46).

Question 7. You may get a wide variety of opinions on this question, and you will probably not arrive at a definitive answer. Some Christians believe that the same authenticating, miraculous works of the early church should be seen today as evidence of the Spirit's presence. Other Christians believe that the message of the gospel is authenticated today by the quiet work of the Spirit in those who believe. You can explore these issues further by reading my book *Miracles: What the Bible Really Says* (InterVarsity Press). For a different viewpoint look at John White's *When the Spirit Comes with Power* (InterVarsity Press).

Question 8. The miracles of Jesus and the apostles were not performed primarily to meet human needs or to dazzle a crowd. The miracles were God's seal of approval on the messengers and on their message.

Question 9. Opinions will cover a wide range. If a person believes that authenticating miracles were largely confined to the early church era, that person will expect fewer (or no) such miracles today. Those who believe that authenticating miracles are still available will expect to see as many or more miracles today. My personal conviction, based on the pattern of miraculous activity in biblical history, is that public, spectacular miracles were designed to authenticate God's message. Today God works primarily through his providential care and what I call "family miracles"—miracles designed to care for those who have believed on Christ. You may want to continue pondering this question as you do more of the studies in this guide.

Question 11. We tend to give the word *miracle* a broad range of meaning. The Bible uses a much narrower focus. A miracle is a demonstration of God's power that points to God's greater glory and that always produces a sense of wonder in those who experience or hear about the miracle.

Study 2. Supernatural Wonders in a Scientific Age. Exodus 14:5-31.

Purpose: To examine God's power to help his people by intervening miraculously in the created world.

Question 1. Guide the group through the events of the passage as you discuss this question.

Question 3. God's miraculous works always reveal aspects of God's character to those who are willing to see with believing eyes. Moses challenged the people to overcome their normal fear and in faith to see what God would do.

Question 6. Even in the destruction of the Egyptian army God revealed his glory in several ways: (1) by bringing judgment on those who had rebelled against him, (2) by keeping his promises of deliverance to Israel and devastation to Egypt, (3) by showing his reality against the false gods of Egypt, and (4) by demonstrating his power to save his people out of the most desperate circumstances. God hardened the hearts of those who had already hardened their own hearts in unbelief.

Question 7. Some readers of this account explain the escape of the

Israelites on a series of fortuitous natural events. They came to a relatively shallow, marshy area of the Red Sea that allowed human passage but in which the heavy chariots sank; the strong wind drove back the water or held back a tide; a thick fog made it impossible for the Egyptians to see while the Israelites made their way across the wet swamp.

Other elements point to a supernatural source for their escape. They walked on dry ground not marshy ground; a wall of water stood on each side of the Israelites; the water killed all the Egyptians not merely bringing them to a halt.

Question 8. God used the participation of Moses to single him out as God's chosen spokesman and leader. Periods of intense miraculous activity in biblical history were usually designed to point out one person or one group as God's representative.

Question 9. Encourage the group to think about God's rescue in more than physical terms. The New Testament makes it clear that God has delivered us out of Satan's kingdom by the same power that parted the Red Sea and raised Jesus from the dead! See Ephesians 1:18-20 and Colossians 1:13.

Study 3. Jesus the Miracle Worker. Luke 7:11-23.

Purpose: To show Jesus as the one able to work miraculously in our lives.

Question 2. John apparently was looking for the same kind of deliverer that many others were expecting—a political redeemer who would quickly establish a visible kingdom. I am sure the imprisonment of a righteous man was not part of the vision John had of the age the Messiah would usher in. Perhaps John was trying by his question to urge Jesus to take more dramatic action.

Question 3. Jesus responded by performing the very acts the prophets had said would mark the coming of Israel's Savior. See, for example, Isaiah 29:18-19; 35:3-6; 61:1-2.

Question 4. Jesus always responded to sincere questions with patience and compassion. He lets us wrestle with our doubts until we are willing to listen to his words and submit to his will.

Question 5. Jesus not only pointed to his miracles to reassure John, but he gave a promise that John would be blessed by God if he continued to trust Jesus even when circumstances made trust difficult. Jesus did not come to earth simply to fulfill John's expectations (or ours!). He came to do the

Father's will. God doesn't always explain the details of his plan to us. He calls us to trust in him even when we cannot see what he is doing.

Question 7. Jesus' miracles were designed primarily to authenticate himself as the Messiah of Israel and God's chosen spokesman. Other purposes for his miracles emerge from this passage too—the miracles visualized the blessings of a new age; the miracles relieved human suffering; the miracles assured believers of God's presence and power.

Question 8. Some in your group will think that an outpouring of miracles would produce revival and waves of conversions. But Jesus performed hundreds of public miracles during his ministry, and in the end only a few genuinely believed on him. Other people will say that an abundance of miracles would do virtually nothing to impress our society. But one miracle in Acts 3 (Peter and John heal a lame man) stirred such interest that a multitude listened to the gospel and hundreds believed!

Question 9. These questions have no *definitive* answer. The purpose of asking them is to get your group to wrestle with the issues and implications of each position. Any conclusions should be based on Scripture, not simply on personal impressions.

Study 4. Power in the Presence of Death. Luke 8:40-42, 49-56.

Purpose: To demonstrate God's ability to conquer even the most fearful situation we can imagine.

Introduction. The eight people raised from the dead were a child raised to life by Elijah (1 Kings 17:17-24), a child raised by Elisha (2 Kings 4:32-37); a man buried with Elisha's bones (2 Kings 13:20-21), Jairus' daughter (the passage in this study), the son of a widow in the city of Nain (Lk 7:11-15), Jesus' friend Lazarus (Jn 11:1-44), Dorcas raised by Peter (Acts 9:36-42), and Eutychus raised by Paul (Acts 20:7-12). These miracles revived the person back to normal human life. Jesus, in contrast, was resurrected in a glorified body to a new kind of life.

Group discussion. If you'd rather not get into the near-death controversy, you might ask, "How far would you go to bring physical healing or help to someone you love?"

Question 1. The story of the raising of Jairus' daughter is also found in Mark 5:21-24, 35-43 and Matthew 9:18-19, 23-26.

Question 2. Some interpreters believe that the girl was in a coma—a deep "sleep." Jesus even said she was asleep (v. 52) and assured Jairus that she would be "healed" rather than "raised" (v. 50). The most definitive statement, however, is Luke's comment that "her spirit returned" to her body, a clear indication that she had died. Jesus sometimes used "sleep" as a figure of physical death (see, for example, Jn 11:11-14). He may have used it here because the girl's death was temporary, like a night's sleep.

Question 4. Sometimes faith plays a vital part in the accomplishment of a biblical miracle; at other times faith is not mentioned or is impossible. In this situation Jesus is urging Jairus to trust Jesus even when the situation seems hopeless.

Question 5. Jairus' house was filled with professional mourners, people hired to add volume to the family's grief over the death of a loved one. The lack of sincerity is demonstrated by their ability to change from wailing to laughter almost immediately.

Question 6. Jesus did not spend a lot of time seeking to convince those who rudely dismissed his capacity to do mighty works. He had patience with people who were struggling with sincere doubt but refused to cast the pearls of his wisdom before those who blatantly hardened their minds and hearts. Skeptics should be answered with a challenge to their unbelief and a presentation of the gospel rather than with long attempts at intellectual persuasion.

Question 7. Apparently Jesus sensed that this was not an appropriate time to draw further public attention to his ministry. Perhaps Jesus knew that his growing popularity with the people and the increasing opposition from the religious leaders would spark a crisis before his ministry was completed.

Question 8. A believer who dies is "with Christ" in a place which is "better by far" than this earthly realm (Phil 1:23). We may grieve over our temporary separation, but we look forward to our reunion, not to their return to life.

Question 10. We usually think we know exactly what God should do to rescue us or to straighten out a difficult situation. What pleases him most, however, is when we put aside our fear and trust him to work as he desires and when he desires.

Study 5. Rebuking Satan's Power. Luke 8:26-39.

Purpose: To gain assurance of Jesus' power over any evil enemy standing against us.

General note. This study needs to be approached with a prepared and protected heart and mind. Sometimes the study of Satan and his demons can open an unhealthy curiosity about their power. It would be wise to begin the study with prayer. Ask God for his protection over the group. During the study, point out the surpassing power of Jesus Christ over all the power of evil.

Question 3. Jesus tried to help this man by confronting the true cause of the problem. The people of the area had simply tried to control or contain the man.

Question 4. The man today would undoubtedly be declared mentally deranged, and attempts would be made to institutionalize (contain) or medicate (control) him.

Question 5. Throughout his ministry Jesus talked about, talked to and responded to actual beings called demons or evil spirits. He never gave any indication that these beings were merely figments of human imagination or convenient explanations for mental illness. The Bible describes demons as powerful but sinful angels who operate under the direction of Satan, "the prince of demons."

Question 6. The New Testament writers speak clearly of attacks upon Christians by Satan and his demons (Eph 6:10-13; 1 Jn 4:1-3). Demons may not demonstrate their presence as crudely in our culture as they did in Jesus' day, but they are still at work deceiving the world and seeking to defeat believers.

Question 7. If appropriate to the comfort level of your group, you might want to ask a follow-up question: "Have you ever wanted Jesus to leave you alone? Why?"

Question 8. Jesus realized that this man needed time for spiritual recovery and growth—and one of the ways to cultivate spiritual maturity is to get involved in ministry. The man went through the whole city telling about Jesus' power to liberate people in bondage. In Mark's account (Mk 5:20) we are told that the man expanded his evangelistic ministry to the whole region.

Question 9. Opinions on the Christian's authority over demons will vary. Encourage those who respond to have a clearly *biblical* basis for their belief and not just what they have been told or have come to believe.

Question 10. Christians need to realize that demons have incredible power and are not to be treated lightly. Christ is the one who has conquered every evil foe (Col 2:15), and we appeal to *his* name and *his* authority to rebuke evil forces (Jude 8-9). The obedient Christian walking in the Spirit has little to fear from demonic oppression. Jesus himself prays to the Father for our protection from the evil one (Jn 17:15; see also 2 Thess 3:3; 1 Jn 5:18).

Question 11. You may want to close this study with prayer. Specifically ask God to guard your minds and your spirits against demonic influence or attack.

Study 6. When Our Efforts Fail. Mark 9:14-29.

Purpose: To demonstrate the wisdom of always relying on God's power rather than on our own resources.

Question 2. The disciples had been with Jesus long enough to witness many exorcisms, or the casting out of demons. They probably tried all the outward things they had seen Jesus do: calling the demon out, rebuking the demon, laying hands on the boy. They went through outward motions but without a source of genuine spiritual power.

Question 4. Jesus includes the disciples with the entire "unbelieving generation" to which he spoke. The disciples were trying to do God's work by using purely secular techniques. They were acting like the unbelieving society around them. Jesus calls them back to a reliance on the power of God. Faith is trusting God's ability to do what he promises. It is an acknowledgment of our inability and God's total ability. The father was trusting in the disciples; the disciples were trusting in their position or personal ability. Both the father and the disciples needed a reawakening to the complete powerlessness of their own efforts in the spiritual realm.

Question 7. Some Christians have misused verse 23 to explain why other sincere Christians have not been healed or delivered from a difficult situation. "If you had more faith," they are told, "the miracle would come." Faith is certainly a vital element in the Christian life. God may, however, choose not to heal a believer who is sick. It is not a lack of faith but the sovereign decision of a loving Father. When Jesus was unable to do miracles in his home town of Nazareth, for example, it was because the people exhibited *no* faith in him, not because they needed more faith (Mt 13:58; Mk 6:5-6).

Question 8. Jesus' response was not to rebuke the father for a lack of faith but to nurture and encourage the seed of faith beginning to unfold. The father's request for Jesus help to overcome his unbelief was answered as Jesus drew him deeper in his reliance on Christ alone for his son's deliverance.

Question 9. Resting the full weight of our problems on the Lord and trusting him to work in our lives can bring a sense of fear and insecurity. We have tried to handle them ourselves for so long that we feel strange giving them to the Lord. Jesus often waits, however, until we give the burden to him before he works to bring a change in the situation.

If you have not already discussed this, you might ask the group, "What are some circumstances in which you might be tempted to trust your own wisdom and ability rather than the wisdom and power of God?"

Question 10. Jesus was not saying that there was just one more thing the disciples should have done. Prayer is the admission that we can't do anything to change a particular situation and, if anything will be done, God has to do it. Jesus was pointing out again the disciples' powerlessness in the spiritual realm when they rely simply on their own wisdom and resources.

Study 7. Facing an Impossible Situation. John 6:1-15.

Purpose: To awaken in us a new awareness of Jesus' willingness and ability to meet our needs.

Question 1. This miracle is usually referred to as the feeding of the five thousand. John does say in verse 10 that "the men sat down, about five thousand of them." Matthew adds that the figure did not include women and children (Mt 14:21). Many evangelical scholars estimate the size of the crowd to have been about fifteen thousand people.

Question 2. Jesus often used real life situations and problems to build faith in his disciples. Challenge those in your group to use life's difficulties as opportunities to build trust toward God in those they are seeking to disciple (their children, for example, or new believers or younger leaders in ministry).

Question 3. Philip tended to calculate how to get himself out of a difficult situation. Andrew's approach was to say, "What's the use?" and give up. Our responses seem to fall to one extreme or the other (with variations). If you are constrained by time, you may want to limit the sharing to two or three people or ask, "Who in the group responds to difficulty more like Philip (or more like Andrew) responded?"

Question 4. Jesus was trying to get both men to say, "I don't know how to feed this crowd, Lord, but *you* do!"

Question 6. The crowd was intent on making Jesus king because he gave them food to eat (Jn 6:26). When Jesus began to explain the spiritual demands of discipleship, many people turned away (Jn 6:66). The people who ate the miraculous meal were intent on using Jesus to meet their needs; they had no desire to obey him.

Question 7. God may bring us into a difficult situation in order to develop our faith in him. He may allow us to reach the point where we have nothing to lean on but his promises.

Question 9. God may not always change the situation we are in. He may change us in the situation so that we respond differently to it. He may also allow us to remain in a difficult situation, trusting him, in order to use us as the instrument in his hand to change others or to display his grace.

Study 8. "Do You Want To Get Well?" John 5:1-15.

Purpose: To see Jesus' power to heal us.

Question 2. The man had not come or been brought to Jesus seeking healing, nor had he asked Jesus for help. Perhaps the man no longer had the will to be cured. Some interpreters suggest that a few beggars found their life rather easy and even profitable—a lifestyle that would be lost to this man if he were healed.

Question 3. The popular belief was that an angel periodically stirred the water in the pool. The first person in the water after the "stirring" was supposed to be cured of any disease. The movement in the pool was actually caused by a sudden rush of water from an underground spring. Since those with relatively minor ailments could get to the water first, the superstition grew about the pool's magical powers. The man did not see Jesus as a possible source of healing. He was focused only on the water and his inability to get in the pool before others.

Question 6. Often faith played a role in the healing ministry of Jesus, but in this case the man didn't even know who Jesus was. Although Jesus usually healed in response to faith, a person's lack of faith did not limit him either.

Question 7. A person may become sick because of ongoing personal sin. Since Scripture normally pictures sickness as a means of God's chastening in a *believer's* life (see 1 Cor 11:29-31 and Jas 5:16), it is unlikely that the man's sickness was because of unconfessed sin. In the ultimate sense, of course, all sickness is a result of the sinful condition of humanity. What

Jesus may have been emphasizing is the man's need for the new birth and spiritual redemption. The eternal consequences of sin are far worse that any physical sickness or disability.

Question 8. You will again have several different opinions on this question. An important point to remember is that while the character of Jesus never changes, the way he works in our world does change. His miracles on earth were designed to point to him as the Messiah. His miracles today may have a very different purpose, and therefore we may see a different level of miraculous activity.

Question 9. I have outlined five biblical steps to take when you get sick in chapter seven of *Miracles: What the Bible Says*. They are (1) ask God to heal you, (2) seek competent medical help, (3) confess any known sin in your life, (4) ask the spiritual leaders of your church to anoint you in obedience to James 5:14-16, and (5) rest fully in God's care.

Study 9. When the Wrong Seems Strong. Acts 5:17-32.

Purpose: To demonstrate God's powerful involvement in our lives even when evil seems victorious.

Introduction. The story of John and Betty Stam can be found in Mrs. Howard Taylor, *The Triumph of John and Betty Stam* (China Inland Mission, 1935), and in Ruth Tucker, *From Jerusalem to Irian Jaya: A Biographical History of Christian Missions* (Zondervan, 1983), pp. 421-24. Another excellent resource on the persecution of Christians in the twentieth century is James and Marti Hefley, *By Their Blood: Christian Martyrs in the Twentieth Century*, 2nd ed. (Baker, 1996).

Question 1. An interesting speculative question to ask the group is: How did the angel set the apostles free if the guards were still at the doors and the jail was securely locked (v. 23)? We aren't told how it happened but it might spark some interesting discussion.

Question 4. Encourage the people in your group to think carefully about this question and to evaluate their lives honestly. If a person says that Jesus Christ is the ultimate authority but does not demonstrate allegiance to Christ in specific ways, that person needs to reexamine the true sources of authority in his or her life.

Question 7. The persecution, slaughter and imprisonment of believers put our faith to the test more directly than almost any other attack. If we are

God's people, why doesn't he protect us? God has his purposes even in persecution. Often the church grows faster and stronger under persecution than in times of tolerance and peace. We can also be assured that God hears the cry of his suffering people, and in his time he will rescue them.

Question 9. Members of your group may need some help refining their demonstrations of allegiance to Christ. The goal is not to be obnoxious or personally offensive in our commitment but to be courageous in demonstrating our submission to Christ's lordship.

Now or Later. As the leader of the group you may want to come prepared with information or articles about the persecuted church. Web sites, specific organizations or copies of recent articles will help group members get started.

Study 10. Deceptive Miracles & Miracle Workers. Matthew 7:15-27.

Purpose: To be alerted to the enemy's power to use miracles to deceive those who are undiscerning.

Question 1. The main contrasts are between wolves and sheep, good trees and bad trees, and a wise man and a foolish man. In each case it is difficult at first to tell the difference between the good and the bad. Followers of Christ have to use clear judgment and sound principles to unmask those who would lead us astray.

Question 2. In verse 1 of Matthew 7 Jesus is talking about judging others in regard to our own prejudices and opinions. In his command to watch for false prophets, he is calling us to make judgments based on biblical principles. Christians *should* make judgments on issues clearly set down in Scripture (see 1 Thess 5:21; 1 Jn 4:1; 1 Cor 14:29).

Question 3. "Fruit" includes the outward results of someone's ministry but extends also to the person's character and their loyalty to biblical truth.

Question 4. The people who stand before the Lord seem to confess Jesus as Lord ("Lord, Lord") and do great works of power in his name and under his authority.

Question 5. In spite of their confession and testimony of miracles, Jesus will see the reality of their hearts. These people had simply attached the name of Jesus to their own attempts at religious influence. Their miracles had their source in Satan's power, not in God's, and were performed to deceive those who saw and experienced them.

Some interpreters have tried to say that these individuals had been true believers and had performed genuine miracles in Jesus' name and then had fallen away. That position is refuted, however, by Jesus' statement that he had *never* known them.

Question 6. Jesus said that only those who do the will of his Father will enter the kingdom of heaven. The will of God encompasses inner transformation and personal purity (1 Thess 4:3), control of the Holy Spirit (Eph 5:17-18), and complete obedience to Christ (Rom 12:1-12).

Question 8. What distinguishes the wise person from the foolish person is not just hearing the words of Jesus. They both "hear my words." The wise person, however, "puts them into practice." The true servant of God models a life of obedience and humble service to Christ.

Study 11. Convincing the Skeptic. Matthew 12:22-37.

Purpose: To explore how Jesus responded to critics of his ministry and to learn how we can answer those who are skeptical of Jesus' miracles.

Question 2. The religious leaders were envious of Jesus' influence on the people. They could not deny his miracles; their only hope was to discredit his source of power. "The Son of David" was a term used of the promised Messiah. If Jesus emerged as a deliverer in the minds of the people, the religious leaders risked losing their hold over them.

Question 4. Modern skeptics take one of two approaches to Jesus' miracles. Some try to explain what happened in naturalistic terms. For example, they would say that Jesus did not literally walk on water as his disciples thought but only walked out into the sea on a submerged sandbar. Other skeptics deny any historical basis for the miracles. These stories were made up by the followers of Jesus one or two generations later to support the church's belief in Jesus as God in human flesh. The Christ of faith (they say) is not the same as the Jesus of history.

Question 5. Jesus used three examples to demonstrate that the Pharisee's accusation was totally illogical. (1) If Jesus cast out demons (Satan's angels) by the power of Satan, Satan was fighting against himself. (2) If Jesus drove out demons successfully by Satan's power, how can the Pharisees claim God's power and fail at the same task? (3) No one who is not more powerful than Satan can defeat Satan (the strong man). By tying up the strong man and robbing him of his victims, Jesus was showing himself greater than Satan.

Question 8. The "unpardonable sin" (vv. 31-32) has been a subject of debate since the New Testament was written. One opinion is that it was a specific sin that could only be committed during Jesus' earthly ministry. To see Jesus' miracles and to attribute those miracles to Satan rather than to the Holy Spirit was a sin that cut a person off from redemption. Those who saw Jesus' miracles and still turned their backs on him demonstrate that they have already hardened their hearts against the Lord. Such people cannot be saved because they will not believe.

Question 10. The real problem with those who deny or attack the Bible is not an intellectual problem; it is a spiritual problem. What they need is not to be convinced intellectually but to be changed by God's grace through the gospel. The best approach to a skeptic is a joy-filled, clear witness to what Jesus has done by his death and resurrection and an appeal to that person to believe on Jesus as Savior and Lord.

Question 11. We are not saved by our words; we are saved by grace through faith in Christ. Our words, however, reveal what is really in our hearts (Mt 12:34). Our words will demonstrate whether we are believers in Christ and are therefore acquitted, or whether we are condemned. The fact that we will give an account to God for every careless word should prompt us to seek the Spirit's power to control what we say.

Study 12. When God Says No. 2 Corinthians 12:1-10.

Purpose: To see how we can trust God fully even when the miracle we ask for is not granted.

Question 2. Most interpreters conclude that Paul is talking about himself and his own experiences. He uses indirect language ("I know a man in Christ") to draw attention away from himself. Some students of Paul's letters conclude that he is talking about one of the false apostles who has come to Corinth claiming such a vision of heaven. "I will boast about a man like that," Paul says in mockery, "but I will not boast about myself, except about my weaknesses" (v. 5).

Question 3. Paul's "thorn" was apparently a physical affliction or condition (poor eyesight?) that became a constant reminder that his position as an apostle and the abundance of his visions and revelations came to him purely by God's grace and not because of his own importance.

Question 7. God may not heal us or deliver us from a painful situation, but he has not abandoned us. Furthermore, he will supply sufficient grace to endure the affliction in joyful anticipation of our ultimate deliverance.

Question 10. It is always easy to approach others who are suffering with pat answers and get-out-quick solutions. We model the love of Christ when we stand with the suffering and seek to be one means by which God can supply the grace they need to endure.

Now or Later. You may want to take time for a summary discussion and make a list of principles together.

Douglas Connelly is pastor of Cross Church. Doug and his wife, Karen, live in Flushing, Michigan, with their youngest child, Kyle. Doug is also the author of the LifeGuide(R) Bible Studies Angels, Meeting the Spirit, Daniel, *and* John, *and the books* Angels Around Us, Miracles *and* Mary.

What Should We Study Next?

A good place to start study of Scripture would be with a book study. Many groups begin with a Gospel, such as *Mark* (20 studies by Jim Hoover) or *John* (26 studies by Douglas Connelly). These guides are divided into two parts, so that if twenty or tweny-six weeks seems like too much to do at once, the group can feel free to do half and take a break with another topic. You might want to come back to it later.

You might prefer to try a smaller letter. *Philippians* (9 studies by Donald Baker), *Ephesians* (13 studies by Andrew T. and Phylis J. Le Peau) and *1 & 2 Timothy and Titus* (12 studies by Pete Sommer) are good options. If you want to vary your reading with an Old Testament book, consider *Ecclesiastes* (12 studies by Bill and Teresa Syrios) for a challenging and exciting study.

There are a number of interesting topical *Lifebuilder* studies as well. Here are some options for filling three or four quarters of a year:

Basic Discpleship
Christian Beliefs – 12 studies by Stephen D. Eyre
Christian Character – 12 studies by Andrea Sterk & Peter Scazzero
Christian Disciplines – 12 studies by Andrea Sterk & Peter Scazzero
Evangelism – 12 studies by Rebecca Pippert & Ruth Siemens

Building Community
Christian Community – 12 studies by Rob Suggs
Fruit of the Spirit – 9 studies by Hazel Offner
Spiritual Gifts – 12 studies by Charles & Anne Hummel

Character Studies
New Testament Characters – 12 studies by Carolyn Nystrom
Old Testament Characters – 12 studies by Peter Scazzero
Old Testament Kings – 12 studies by Carolyn Nystrom
Women of the Old Testament – 12 studies by Gladys Hunt

The Trinity
Meeting God – 12 studies by J. I. Parker
Meeting Jesus – 13 studies by Leighton Ford
Meeting the Spirit – 12 studies by Douglas Connelly

ALSO FOR SMALL GROUPS

As well as over 70 titles in the popular *LifeBuilder* series, Scripture Union produces a wide variety of resources for small groups. Among them are:

WordLive – an innovative online Bible experience for groups and individuals, offering a wide variety of free material: study notes, maps, illustrations, images, poems, meditations, downloadable podcasts, prayer activities. Log on and check it out: www.wordlive.org

The Multi-Sensory series – popular resources for creative small groups, youth groups and churches that appeal to a wide range of learning styles.

Deeper Encounter – for confident groups that have a good understanding of Bible text – containing seven studies, complete with CD audio tracks and photocopiable worksheets.

Top Tips on Leading Small Groups – biblical patterns and practical ideas to inspire leaders of small groups.

Essential 100 and *Essential Jesus* – 100-reading overview of the Bible (*Essential 100*) and the person and work of Jesus (*Essential Jesus*), with notes and helps – presented as a programme for individuals, small groups or whole churches.

Small Groups Growing Churches – a flexible training resource for leading small groups. Can be used as a complete 15-topic training course, for a tailor-made church weekend or for one-off refresher sessions.

SU publications are available from Christian bookshops, on the Internet, or via mail order. Advice on what would suit your group best is always available. You can:

- log on to www.scriptureunion.org.uk
- phone SU's mail order line: 01908 856006
- email info@scriptureunion.org.uk
- fax 01908 856020
- write to SU Mail Order, PO Box 5148, Milton Keynes MLO, MK2 2YX

Scripture Union
Using the Bible to inspire children, young people and adults to know God.

Scripture union

100 Essential Readings
through the Bible

E 100

With over 75,000 series sales the
Essential 100 Bible Reading Challenge has
already encouraged hundreds of Christians
to meet God every day through the Bible.

With **100 carefully selected Bible passages,**
50 Old Testament and 50 New Testament,
the E100 readings are designed to give a
good understanding of the overall Bible
story from Genesis to Revelation.

Single book:	5-pack also available:
978 1 84427 566 3	978 1 84427 546 5
£6.99	£25.00

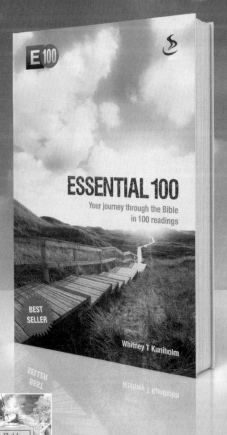

ESSENTIAL 100
Your journey through the Bible
in 100 readings

BEST
SELLER

Whitney T Kuniholm

ESSENTIAL JESUS

Single book:
978 184427 238 9
£6.99

5-pack also available:
978 184427 239 6
£25.00

Big Bible
Challenge

Single book:
978 1 84427 584 7
£9.99

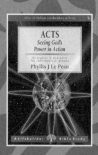

Have you ever asked yourself

How can I make a difference for God?

On some level, we all struggle to find our own answer to that fundamental question. The search for significance is the underlying motivation for virtually all human activity. It's what drives us.

The Essential Question takes you on a journey through the book of Acts. Fifty Bible readings to help you begin to find and follow God's plan for you today.

Single book:	5-pack also available:
978 1 84427 902 9	978 1 84427 903 6
£6.99	£25.00

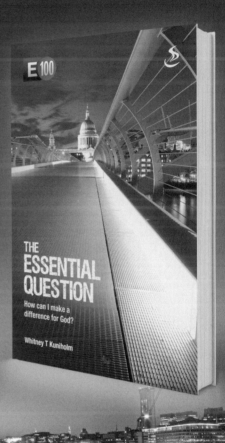

ESSENTIAL 100

Single book:
978 1 84427 566 3
£6.99

5-pack also available:
978 1 84427 546 5
£25.00

ESSENTIAL JESUS

Single book:
978 184427 238 9
£6.99

5-pack also available:
978 184427 239 6
£25.00

Single book:
978 1 84427 584 7
£9.99

SCAN HERE
FOR MORE INFO